Queen of the Concrete Jungle

BY Erika London

ILLUSTRATED BY Mike Essa

JEMM Publishing

Illustrations by Mike Essa
Graphic Design by Alexis Carranza

ISBN 9780578889146

www.erikalondon.com

To all the NYC mamas —
I see you. I hope this book captures a piece of your NYC magic and a time where whether you knew it or not, you were not only a NYC Mom but also Queen of the best city in the world.

To my Mom (the original *Queen of the Concrete Jungle*) — thanks for being proof that you can leave NYC but it never leaves you and that with your Mom's love and support, you can do anything.

To my girls — I hope you remember the magic and find yourselves being pulled back into it one day.

To my husband — thank you for being our King, my rock and the most supportive human ever.

New York City
April

Once upon a time I lived on an island,
the one and only New York City.
There's no place like it in the whole wide world,
it's as beautiful as it is gritty.

A concrete jungle that is so full of life,
home to over 8 million people... it's wild!
Only a Queen like my mom could run it,
with pure magic for every adult and child.

Everyone speaks different languages,
you hear them everywhere you roam.
They come from countries all over the world,
but they all call this city home.

It's filled with so many historic buildings,
so much theater and Broadway.
So many museums and sporting events,
and don't forget the ballet!

A city so nice,
they named it twice,
every adventurous person's
paradise!

Leopards, bears and monkeys in Central Park,
dinosaurs on the Upper West Side.

Puppies and pigeons everywhere you look,
fruit stands for all of them curbside.

Broadway

All hail the queen,
all she has to do is raise her hand.
Taxis and cars rush to her side,
as if they're on demand.

The tallest buildings you've ever seen,
so tall they touch the sky.
The sunshine made them sparkle,
and made you feel like you could fly!

There are so many talented artists
in this NYC bubble.
Mom lets you draw anywhere you want,
and you never get in trouble!

Street art is all around you,
majestic installations everywhere.
Street performers anywhere you look,
as live music flows through the air.

So many artists share their work for free,
and everything is so pretty.
Nothing can compare to this world stage,
this is New York City.

NYC Kids
Rule
Dream
Crayons

Central Park is my own backyard,
hundreds of acres of parks and fun!
A castle, a zoo, and a pond of ducks to feed,
miles of trails to explore and run!

An ice skating rink and a carousel,
playgrounds full of slides.
Sandboxes, waterfalls, picnic spots,
and even horse and carriage rides!

Subway
Imagination Station
A B C 1 2 3
Manhattan
Brooklyn

Our subway ride is so much fun,
it takes you around the rainbow lines.
Get excited, buy a ticket
and follow the ABC & 123 signs.

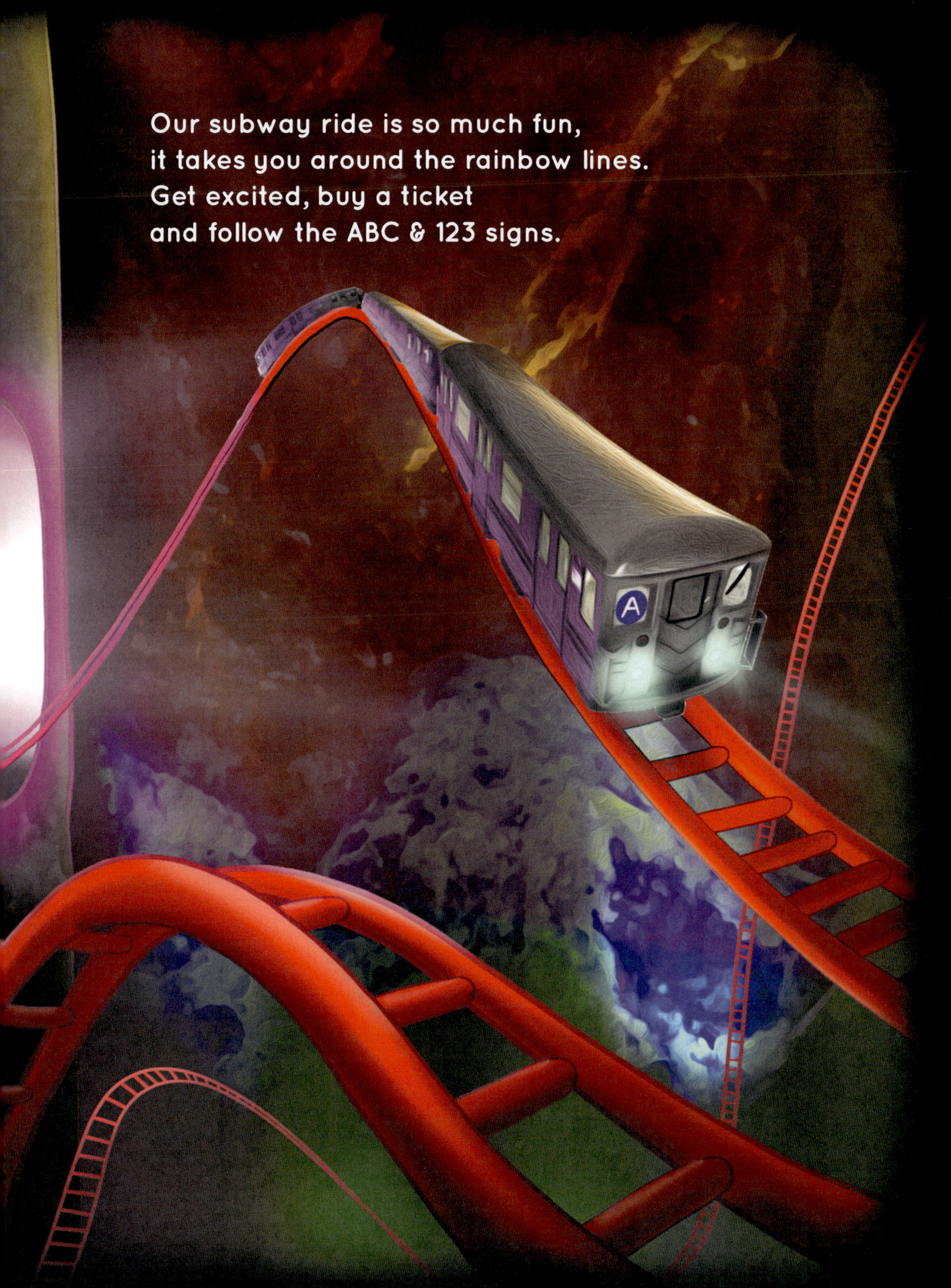

It's definitely not perfect and
sometimes feels like love and hate.
Everyone is always running
and traffic always makes you late.

The streets are always full of people rushing,
talking and being loud.
No matter the time of day or weather,
Mom can always push through a crowd.

It seems like there is always construction
and it could be a little cleaner.
It feels like there is never enough space,
but isn't the grass always greener?

Dressed in her all black momiform,
she can do anything in a New York minute.
On a mission and up for the challenge,
she's always in it to win it.

領先旅遊
二樓
移民入籍
商業信用卡
福利申請
承接裝修工程
SUSHI
by Bou
Falafel Restaurant
PIZZA
Famous PIZZA
PIZZA
Lo Mein
CHINESE FOOD TAKE OUT
Soft Pretzel
Hot Dog
BAGELS
BAGELS

Everything is always on the menu,
and everyone always wants to eat!
The best pizza, bagels, dumplings and pad thai
and you barely have to leave your street.

Iconic food trucks on every corner,
and the most delicious sushi and steak.
The food scene is unparalleled
and no one ever gets a bellyache!

Food carts with hot dogs and soft pretzels,
delis which serve pastrami on rye.
Bodegas have every snack you need,
there is just so much food to try!

All cuisines are available for delivery,
anytime day or night.
The big apple is delicious,
we savor every single bite!

Times Square has the biggest TVs
that you will ever see!
Sometimes Mom says screen time is ok,
for the 50 million tourists and me.

We pretend we're tourists in our own city,
it's so much fun it's not even fair.
It's like Mom always says,
"New York City or nowhere."

Sometimes life feels crazy,
but Mom always has tricks up her sleeve.
The only ball she ever drops,
is the one on New Year's Eve.

2018
ANDY
FOR
ALE
25¢

There is always a celebration,
street fairs and parades.
Fireworks along the river,
the excitement never fades.

The holidays are magical,
ice skating and shopping galore.
The windows are decorated
and come to life at every single store!

The biggest Christmas tree in all the land,
joy for every girl and boy.
The love and magic that you feel all around,
is better than any toy!

NYC never sleeps,
and neither did we.
Too many plans to make,
too many things to do and see.

Anything is possible
in the city that never goes to sleep.
Mom was always up counting dreams,
while we were counting sheep.

NYU

New York City's convenience
and 24/7 hours aren't enough.
You need a mama who's strong,
you need a mama who's tough.

Her hands are full with everything
and her pockets are full of dreams.
She looks like a natural superhero,
but it's not as easy as it seems.

She laughs at balance and she knows
it's more of a juggling act.
She's also the Queen of multi-tasking,
yes that is a fact.

Everything is at her fingertips,
the world in the palm of her hand.
Yet somehow nothing ever goes
exactly as she planned.

She's mastered organized chaos,
the mom juggle is so real.
The hustle and bustle of NYC
makes her even more surreal!

WE ♥ OUR HEROES
MAD
SQ
PK
FDNY
FDNY
NYPD

How does she do it all?
It's because she's not alone.
Her tribe of trusted mom friends
together all share the throne.

They travel with their strollers,
babies always in tow.
In NYC you can take your kids
everywhere you go.

They run on wine and coffee,
there's a magic in their eyes.
They're always texting strategy
between the laughs and cries.

The city is also full of protectors
that keep the people safe and sound.
Doctors and nurses in the hospitals,
police and firefighters all around.

Nothing is impossible and
nothing stands in her way,
when she wakes up in the city that never sleeps,
every, single, day.

She fell in love with New York City
the second it called her name.
Doesn't matter if she stays or goes,
she'll never be the same.

A love like that is forever,
it runs through your veins.
Regardless of the distance,
one simple fact remains.

NYC makes you feel crazy,
it makes you feel whole,
it makes you feel hungry,
it feeds your soul.

This city might be too expensive
but it leaves you feeling richer,
when your cup feels empty
it refills your pitcher.

This city gives you life,
it makes you believe.
You can't forget to take that with you,
whenever you leave.

H&M
I
NY

When it was our time to leave,
my Mom couldn't help but cry.
NYC is a special place,
the big apple of her eye.

She looked back on the glittering skyline
and knew nothing could erase,
the life she lived and memories we made
while living in this mystical place.

My mom will always have a piece
of New York City in her heart.
She'll be a dreamer wherever she goes,
and seek out new adventures for us to start.

It doesn't matter where we are,
my mom will always be my Queen.
I hope wherever you are reading this,
you remember the magic and feel seen.

I ♥ NY

Made in the USA
Coppell, TX
09 May 2021